Through of the Camera

Written by Sue Ledington

North Perth
Westfield Elementary

CONTENTS

Through the Camera Lens	2
Diagnostic Imaging	6
Infrared Imaging	8
CCTV (Closed-Circuit Television)	12
Satellite Images	14
Index	17

PEARSON

THROUGH THE CAMERA LENS

People take pictures for many different reasons. For some people, seeing the world through the lens of a camera is about capturing a moment of time in their life. Photographic images help preserve their memories of special events and the people and places involved. For some people, taking pictures is about exploring the world around them and recording information sometimes unseen by the naked eye.

Photographic images can be used for many purposes. They are one of the most effective forms of communication. They can convey new ideas or information to the viewer.

Some Types of Photography	Purpose
Advertising photography	Sells products and services
Architectural photography	Shows different features of buildings – old and new
Astro-photography	Records images from space
Fashion photography	Shows new trends in clothing, accessories, etc
Forensic photography	Records details at a crime scene or an accident or a disaster that might be used for evidence
Newspaper photography	Tells a story about an event or a situation
Sports photography	Catches the action/events in sports
Wildlife photography	Records wild animals in their day-to-day life

Today, the technology used to take images is so advanced that people can use new ways to explore and examine things unseen by the human eye. Images provide an effective tool for people working, for example, in medical science, space exploration, archaeology, geology, town planning, security and conservation. A visual image can capture a moment in reality and give the viewer the chance to analyse the image carefully.

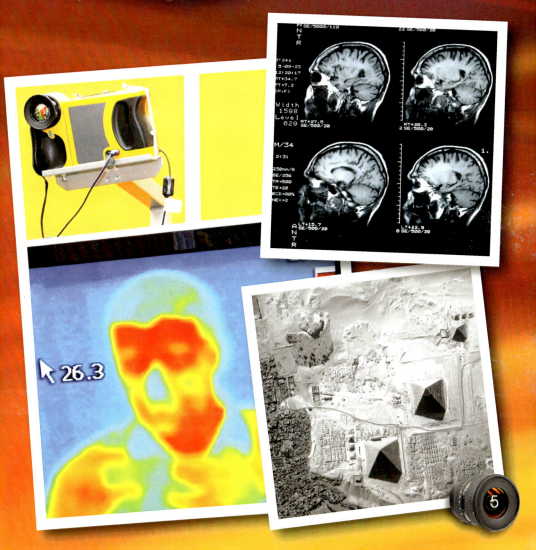

DIAGNOSTIC IMAGING

Diagnostic imaging includes X-rays and scans that help doctors 'see' inside the body and find any problems.

X-rays are mainly used to look for broken bones. An image is produced by X-rays that pass through parts of the body, showing what is inside.

CAT scans examine the whole body, from the brain to the ligaments. A series of images are processed by a computer to provide doctors with a three-dimensional image of the body. Doctors can use the scan to find illnesses, such as cancers.

A doctor examines an X-ray of a person's lungs.

MRI stands for 'magnetic resonance image' and this also provides an accurate and effective way of scanning the body. An image is created on the computer that can then be read by a radiologist.

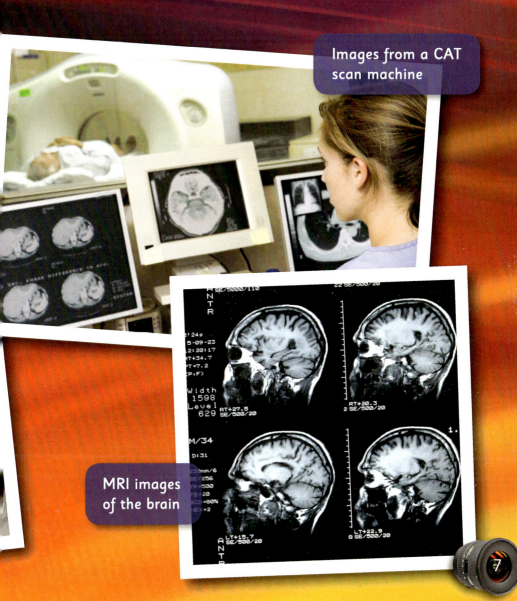

Images from a CAT scan machine

MRI images of the brain

INFRARED IMAGING

Infrared cameras take pictures of heat radiation. In an infrared picture, the hottest areas of the image glow white, bright red and orange; the cooler areas are dark blue, purple and blackish. The ability of these cameras to 'see' heat makes them useful for different purposes.

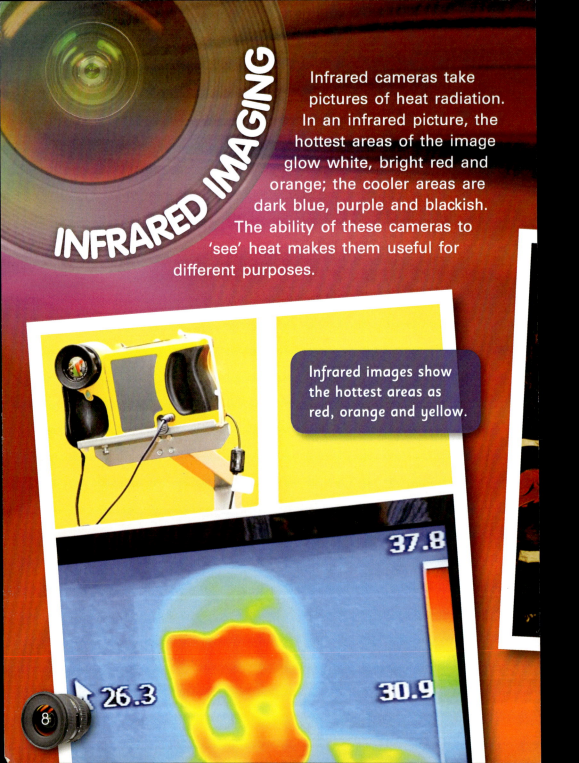

Infrared images show the hottest areas as red, orange and yellow.

37.8

26.3   30.9

Firefighters sometimes use infrared cameras to look for hotspots through smoke, walls and doors. They can find people trapped in smoke-filled buildings.

The police also use infrared cameras, often from helicopters, to chase down criminals in the dark.

Firefighters use an infrared camera to detect heat.

Officials use infrared cameras to check passengers at an airport.

The main benefit of an infrared or a thermal camera is that it can 'see' in the dark. This is why they are used for security purposes. The thermal camera can easily sense night-time intruders. The camera picks out body heat and projects the image on to a screen. Airports and Border Control teams using infrared cameras can monitor from a central base any intruders on their territory. They can track their every move.

Search and Rescue teams sometimes use infrared cameras to help find people lost in the wilderness or at sea. But infrared cameras are used for other purposes too.

The US Navy took this infrared image of a rescue boat while helping to search for survivors of a ferry disaster at night.

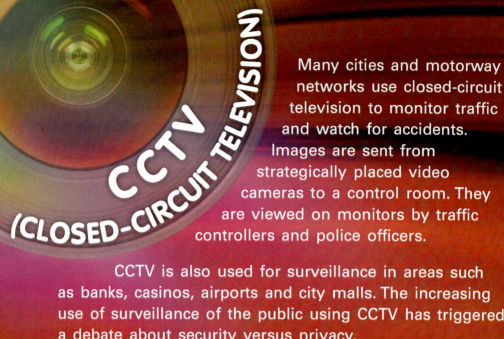

CCTV
(CLOSED-CIRCUIT TELEVISION)

Many cities and motorway networks use closed-circuit television to monitor traffic and watch for accidents. Images are sent from strategically placed video cameras to a control room. They are viewed on monitors by traffic controllers and police officers.

CCTV is also used for surveillance in areas such as banks, casinos, airports and city malls. The increasing use of surveillance of the public using CCTV has triggered a debate about security versus privacy.

In factories, CCTV may be used to prevent accidents by viewing a dangerous process from a central control room. A CCTV system may be installed, too, where an operator of a machine cannot directly see people who might get in the way of the machine. For example, on a subway train, CCTV cameras may help the driver to see that people are clear of doors before closing them and starting the train.

Operators of an amusement park ride may use a CCTV system to check that starting a ride does not endanger people.

Security guards looking at CCTV monitors in the control room

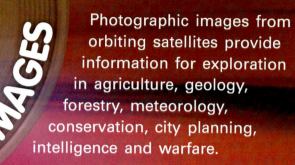

SATELLITE IMAGES

Photographic images from orbiting satellites provide information for exploration in agriculture, geology, forestry, meteorology, conservation, city planning, intelligence and warfare.

Satellite pictures are also used in seismology and oceanography. The cameras can show changes to land forms, water depth and the seabed caused by earthquakes, volcanoes, and tsunamis.

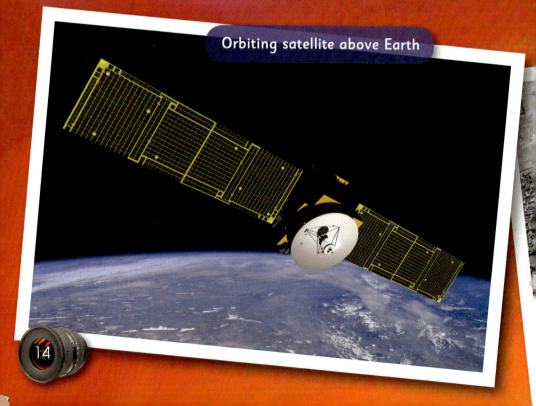

Orbiting satellite above Earth

Using infrared images taken by satellites 700 kilometres above Earth, archaeologists have found several buried pyramids in Egypt. The images also revealed ancient lost tombs and buildings submerged in sand from the time of the Pharaohs. Archaeologists working on these sites found by satellites will now be able to protect and preserve them.

This satellite image shows Hurricane Irene on the east coast of the United States.

This satellite image shows the pyramids in Egypt.

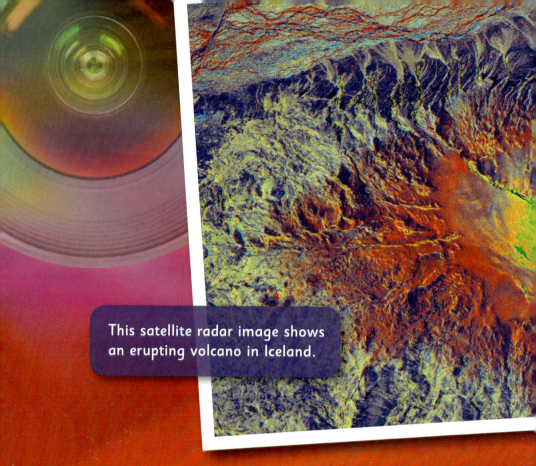

This satellite radar image shows an erupting volcano in Iceland.

Photographic images received from orbiting satellites allow people to monitor the environmental effects, for example, of:
- Volcanic activity
- Natural disasters
- Oil spills
- Climate change
- Water pollution
- Drought and floods
- Industrial waste pollution
- Deforestation

Through the camera lens, people can work towards protecting and preserving the Earth's environments.

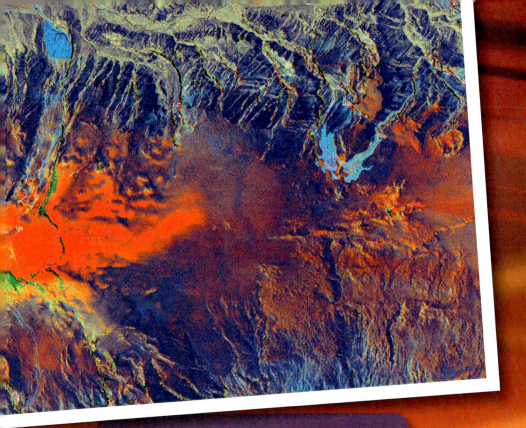

Index

CAT scans	6–7
CCTV	12–13
infrared	8–11, 15
MRI	7
satellite images	14–16
using images in	
medicine	6–7
science	4–5, 14–16
security	10–13
X-rays	6

Informational Report

Informational Reports record factual information about a specific topic

How to Write an Informational Report

Step One

- Select a topic.
- Write down the things you know about the topic.
- Write down the things you need to find out.

> **Through the Eye of the Camera — Research Brief**
> Why do people take pictures, and how do they use the images?
> What different sorts of images are there?
> What kinds of images do X-rays and CAT or MRI scans take?
> What are these images used for?
> What do infrared cameras record?
> What are the images used for?
> What do CCTV cameras record?
> What are the images used for?
> What do satellite cameras record?
> What are the images used for?

Step Two

- Locate the information you need.
- Use different kinds of resources for your investigation:

Internet   Library   Television documentaries

- Take notes or make copies of what you find.

Step Three

Sort through your notes. Organise your information using headings.

Infrared Imaging

Takes pictures of heat radiating from bodies or other objects

Shows the hottest areas in white, or bright red and orange

Shows the coolest in dark blue, purple and blackish

Images are used by:
firefighters to find hot spots or find people trapped in buildings
search and rescue to find people lost in bush or at sea

Step Four

Use your notes to write your Report.

Include an **introduction** with an opening statement:

People take pictures for many different reasons. For some people, seeing the world through the lens of a camera is about capturing a moment of time in their life. Photographic images help people preserve their memories of special events and the people and places involved. For some people, taking pictures is about exploring the world around them and recording information sometimes unseen by the naked eye.

Include **visuals** such as:

Captions   Labels   Photographs   Chart

Your Report could have...

a Contents page

CONTENTS

Through the Camera Lens	2
Diagnostic Imaging	6
Infrared Imaging	8
CCTV (Closed-Circuit Television)	12
Satellite Images	14
Index	17

an Index

Index

CAT scans 6–7
CCTV 12–13
infrared 8–11, 15
MRI.. 7
satellite images 14–16
using images in
    medicine 6–7
    sciencey 4–5, 14–16

Some reports also have a Glossary.

Guide Notes

> **Title: Through the Eye of the Camera**
>
> **Stage:** Advanced Fluency
>
> **Text Form:** Informational Report
>
> **Approach:** Guided Reading
>
> **Processes:** Thinking Critically, Exploring Language, Processing Information
>
> **Written and Visual Focus:** Labels, Captions, Index, Photographs, Contents Page, Chart

THINKING CRITICALLY

(sample questions)

Before Reading – Establishing Prior Knowledge
- What do you know about the different types of images taken through the camera lens and the purposes they are used for?

Visualising the Text Content
- What might you expect to see in this book?
- What form of writing do you think will be used by the author?
- Look at the Contents page and Index. Encourage the students to think about the information and make predictions about the text content.

After Reading – Interpreting the Text
- What do you think is the purpose of this book?
- How does the introduction text on page 2–3 explain the idea behind the topic?
- What sorts of things do you think might be unseen by the human eye?
- Look at pages 4–5. What other areas of work or purposes do you think people might use photographic images for?
- What do you think are the benefits of using medical imaging to detect problems?
- What inferences can you make about other situations where infrared imaging might be useful?
- What is your opinion about the use of CCTV cameras in modern society? Do you think the concerns about the rights of people to privacy are justified? Why or why not?
- How would you find out more about the ways in which satellite images are used? What questions would you formulate for a research brief for this?
- What inferences can you make about the way the photographic images of oil spills might be used?
- What inferences can you make about how people might use the satellite images showing deforestation?
- What questions do you have after reading the text?
- Do you think the author effectively conveyed the information in this book? Why or why not?

EXPLORING LANGUAGE

Terminology
Photograph credits, index, ISBN number, contents page, chart